OUTLINING

STEP-BY-STEP

Essential Chapter Outline, Fiction and Nonfiction Outlining Tricks Any Writer Can Learn

Sandy Marsh

reparation, damages, or monetary loss due to the information herein, either directly or indirectly.

Respective authors own all copyrights not held by the publisher.

The information herein is offered for informational purposes solely, and is universal as so. The presentation of the information is without contract or any type of guarantee assurance.

The trademarks that are used are without any consent, and the publication of the trademark is without permission or backing by the trademark owner. All trademarks and brands within this book are for clarifying purposes only and are the owned by the owners themselves, not affiliated with this document.

Table of Contents

Introduction

Congratulations on purchasing this book and thank you for doing so. The following chapters will teach you all the important things that you need to know about making an outline. Learning to make an effective outline is an invaluable tool as a writer. It can help the writing of your book to flow more smoothly, work out more conveniently and be organized.

Chapter 1 talks about the basics of making an outline. This will give you a good foundation and understanding of what outlining is all about. Chapter 2 discusses how you can make an outline for a fiction book. Chapter 3 teaches how you can make an outline for a non-fiction book. Chapter 4 lays down the best practices that you should observe when making an outline.

Writing a book can be a daunting task. By using an outline, you can make the process of writing a book simpler and easier. The good news is that it is not hard to make an outline as long as you know what you are doing. An outline is an effective tool and is the secret behind an effective book writing. By learning how to make an outline, you are able to cover a significant part of the actual book-making process. Take the outline as a blueprint, the guide, or architecture, of your book.

Chapter 1: The Basics of Making an Outline

What is an outline?

An outline works as a guide when it comes to writing your book. Take note that a book is a big world. Without a good outline, you can easily get lost in the process of writing your book. An outline ensures that you stay within the plot that you want for your book and that every scene works towards building your story.

It is worth noting that an outline only serves as a guide. A writer has the option whether or not to stick to their outline. Still, having an outline is helpful because it will give you a sense of direction. It is also a useful tool to use to ensure proper sequencing of events or scenes in your book.

There are different ways to make an outline. This book will teach you notable and effective methods to outline a book, both for a fiction book and a non-fiction book. Indeed, learning how to make an outline is an invaluable tool that should be in the arsenal of every writer.

It can be said that an outline is the book itself but in a very simplified version. It can also deal with the technical aspects of the book, such as the timing as to when and how a certain characters or ideas will be presented. Consider the outline as the blueprint or the foundational architecture of your book.

Who uses an outline?

Almost all professional writers use an outline. Some go as far as saying that all writers *should* use an outline. The use of an outline does not just refer to books, but even in other forms of writing. In fact, it is not uncommon even for article writers to write an outline for their more complicated articles. An outline ensures that the focus of your writing and the proper flow remain concentrated. So, if making an outline is really this important, are there known authors who apply them? The answer is yes. Here are some examples to name a few: The author of *Harry Potter*, JK Rowling, James Salter, Paulo Coelho, Sylvia Plath, Jennifer

Egan, William Faulkner, and many other popular writers have admitted the use of outlines in the creation of their works. As you can see, using an outline is considered such an essential skill and tool of a writer that even well-known authors use it regularly.

Should you use an outline? Well, just because you are a writer does not necessarily mean that you are required to make an outline before writing your book. So, whether you want to use an outline or not is a matter of personal preference. Still, it is worth noting that many writers have realized the benefits of using an outline.

The importance of using an outline

It is worth noting that there are some authors who do not use an outline when they write a book. Instead, they simply allow the natural current of the work to drive them to somewhere, hoping that it would be worth telling. However, the truth is that many of these of authors have outlined the book in their mind, so somehow, they still have that sense of direction. Of course, there are also those writers who completely have no idea of what they are writing and just see where the writing goes. After all, when it comes to writing, especially when it comes to writing fiction, there are no hard and fast rules to limit a writer. You are free to write your book in whatever way you want just as you are also free not to write a book. However, if you want to be sure of your sense of direction and not waste your time writing on so many pages only to realize that they do not make sense, then you should use an outline. An outline is also easy to make, yet it will assure you that your book has a good flow and direction.

Now, there are those who say that using an outline will only limit your imagination, so they do not want to use an outline when they write a book. They do not want the outline to "cage" the expression and flow of their ideas. However, this is not the correct way to view an outline. Take note that as a writer, an outline is still just an outline. You are not in any way compelled to follow your outline all of the time. For example, let us say while you are writing the setting of the story as stated in your outline you realize that a different place would be more suitable, then you are free to use that place instead of what is in your outline. Of course, the same principle applies to the other parts of the book.

Again, an outline is a helpful guide that will ensure to give you a sense of direction; it should not, in any way, be seen as an obstacle or a cage that limits your imagination. You are strongly encouraged to stretch and explore the beauty of your mind. In fact, even an outline comes from the creative mind of a writer. The outline can be thought of as the skeleton of the book that you hang the actual story on.

Outlining for fiction vs. Non-fiction

Outlining works for any kind of book, whether fiction or non-fiction. However, making an outline for a fiction book is not the same when you make an outline for a nonfiction book and vice versa. This is because of the inherent differences between the two genres. In a fiction book, for example, a novel, you will need to spend more time outlining the plot of the story and the sequencing of the events.

You should be able to present your characters effectively and build up the story. In the case of a non-fiction book, there is usually no need to build up any story. Instead, you should focus on presenting the right information. Of course, the proper sequence should also be observed. In a fiction book, the outline will be mostly composed of the setting, the characters, and the different events that take place in the story. In a non-fiction book, the outline will be divided into main topics and subtopics regarding technical subjects.

Although there are differences between making an outline for fiction and nonfiction, the use and purpose of an outline still remain the same, and that is to make writing the book easier and more organized.

Plot outline vs. synopsis

Many people use these two terms interchangeably. However, it is worth noting that they are not the same. Take note that when you create a plot outline before even start writing a book you then use the outline as your guide as you write, so that you will be guided on how the story should flow. Writers who use plot outlines are usually called "plotters" since they plot the whole story before they even write it down. This is a good way to avoid writing too many drafts with rejected scenes and pages.

A synopsis is usually written after the completion of the book. It refers to the summary of your story or novel. The synopsis is usually a part of a proposal letter that a writer sends to a potential publisher.

A synopsis can be as short as a single page or even up to five pages. A plot outline can also take a single page but can be longer than five pages. It depends on how much you work on your outline. If you add in more details, then it will be able to guide you once you proceed to write your story. In addition to the story, a plot outline can include a detailed character story and other events.

Some writers already know their story before they even write it. So, if you can come up with the synopsis first, then you can use that as a guide to make a more detailed outline.

Understand the plot of a story

If you are into fiction writing, then it is important for you to know the plot of a story. What is a plot? It is what draws readers into the story. It refers to the arrangement of the story elements. There are generally five parts of a plot: the beginning or exposition, rising action, climax, falling action, and denouement or ending. Let us take a look at them one by one.

Exposition

The exposition is the beginning of a story. Hence, this is the part where you present your characters. Take note that the characters are not the only ones that develop your story. You also need to pay attention to the place, as well as the time. Unfortunately, some people forget about the element of time. Do not forget that Paris today was much different a hundred years ago. It is also important to keep the exposition as interesting as possible. You need to make it grab the interest of your readers; otherwise, they might stop reading your book before they even find out the about good and exciting parts.

Rising action

This is where you build up your story. This is usually where a problem is presented, and the characters take steps to face or solve the problem. This is also what prepares the most exciting part of the story, the climax. The rising action is where you build up the anxiety and the expectations. This is also the part where you start to tug at the hearts and emotions of your readers. The more attached the readers are to the characters, the more powerful the climax and the overall story will be. It is important that a writer build up the story effectively; otherwise, the story may become boring to the reader.

Climax

This is known as the turning point and the most exciting part of the story. This is where the emotions are at their peak. Nothing is ever the same as this point. This is where real and solid changes take place. Usually, immediately right after the climax, everything takes a downhill, relaxes, and prepares for the ending.

Falling action

This is the part where the story falls and takes a downhill, which leads to the ending of the story. Here, the story usually comes together, and the missing pieces are finally resolved. This is also where you reward your audience. Take note that your readers normally associate themselves with the protagonist in the story, so you use this part show them how the protagonist is rewarded for all of his or her labor. This is also a good part to impress on the readers the moral of your story if any.

Denouement

This is the ending of the story. Here, the loose ends are tied, and the questions are finally answered. Of course, it can be a happy ending or a sad ending. A story can even have an open ending where there is technically no end and you leave to the reader the final conclusion of the story.

Why is it important to understand the plot?

As a writer, it is important for you to understand the plot. When you make an outline, you actually work on the plot of your story, such as how are you going to begin the story, how do you present your characters, the time and place, etc. before then you moving on to the rising action, then the climax, and so on. As you can see, it is important to have a good understanding of the plot because the story revolves around the plot that you set. There are also writers who make an outline by simply filling in the parts of the plot with details.

Chapter 2: Fiction Outline

Snowball Method

The snowball method is one of the most popular techniques for making an outline. Just like a rolling snowball that gets bigger and bigger as it rolls downhill, the snowball method starts with just a simple topic, idea, or a scene. It will then be continuously developed, and it will branch out to more ideas, more scenes, and other parts of the story.

For example, let's start with the simple idea of a man who falls in love with a woman. Let this idea be the very center of the snowball. This will also be the main theme of the story. We now branch out a little and give them each a name. Let us say that the name of the man is Jack and the name of the woman is Mina. So now we have the protagonists of the story, as well as the central theme of love. Of course, Jack cannot just fall in love with Mina out of nowhere. So, we add another part to our snowball: let us say for example that Mina is in need of money. She then applies for a job at a nearby restaurant which happens to be owned by Jack. Let us say that Mina is able to get the job as a waitress, and she then works as a waitress gets to meet other people who work at the restaurant. Again, this is another part of the snowball.

When working as a waitress, one day, Mina encounters a very rude customer. Again, we let the snowball turn, and we simply continue to add more information or details. For example, let us say that the rude customer is the one who complains and calls for the manager of the restaurant who happens to be Jack as well, the owner. Jack then is able to put the situation under control. That evening, Jack calls Mina to his office for a meeting. Mina is anxious about it because she does not want to lose her job. Again, we simply let the snowball turn and gather more details. Contrary to what she has expected, once she is already in the office, Jack appears to be very polite and even apologizes for what happened that day.

This is simply how the snowball method works. Simply put, you just have to keep adding more and more details. If you continue to do this, then you will soon come up with a short story, a novelette, or even a novel. From one small snowball, you simply let it roll and roll and gather more ideas and details to turn it into a big snowball, a complete story. Also, do not forget that you are writing an outline and not a story just yet. So, keep it simple and short, but be sure that the main points of the story are there.

Pure summary

As the name implies, a pure summary outline is the kind of outline that is composed of summaries. This is like the short version of your entire book or novel. You simply have to summarize everything, such as chapters, scenes, and others.

The idea behind this method is to write down your whole story from beginning to end, but only write down a compressed version. To do this, just write down the important parts or highlights. You can skip all forms of dialogues and just focus on telling what is happening in the story.

For example, Ana is looking for a job and applies as a journalist. She gets the job and as she works as a journalist, she gets to meet Ryan, a photographer, who happens to work in the same company. Despite their busy schedule, they do their best to make time for each other. One day, Ana is in an accident and

Ryan does his best to serve her. To save her life, he has to go into an ancient forest and get a golden apple from a mysterious tree. He ventures into the forest and meets Galdorf, a friendly elf. Galdorf helps him find the mysterious tree and battle the Dark Witch of the forest. By doing so, he frees the imprisoned elves and also saves Ana from dying. They live happily ever after.

As you can see, every part of the story is compressed but it is complete. All that you need to do is to fill in the details. The good thing here is that you are already given a clear roadmap or guideline as to how your story will flow from start to finish. In fact, by using this approach, you will already be able to imagine your story as a whole, and all that you need to do is to write down the details to make the story come alive.

The pure summary is one of the best ways to make an outline. Just summarize every chapter or sub-chapter from beginning to end. When done, you will have a complete story. All that you need to do is to clarify every point by adding in more details.

Skeletal outline

You have probably learned this kind of outline in school or for any other academic purposes. The key to this method is to input the core points in the right order that will best present your story. This is an effective way to get a bird's eye view of your story, including its overall structure. Take note that the structure of a book or story is essential. A book that is poorly structured, whether fiction or non-fiction, will most probably have problems with being disorganized and have confusing contents. A skeletal outline will allow you to easily reform your story or book, which will allow you to create the maximum impact out of your story. Let us take a look at a simple example of a skeletal outline:

Exposition

- The setting of the story takes place in a small village called as Sestin.

- The story introduces Adam, who is a farmer.

- The story then introduces Monica, the daughter of a rich businessman

Rising action

- Adam meets Monica as he tends the farm of her father.

- They get to know each other for some days.

- One day, goblins attack the village of Sestin.

- Monica is held hostage by the goblins.

Climax

- Adam fights the goblins and saves Monica.

- The story also reveals that they both share the same mutual feeling for each other.

- It is found that Adam is actually of royal blood and owns a kingdom

Falling action

- The father of Monica allows Adam to marry his daughter

Denouement

- Adam and Monica get married and everyone is happy.

- They all live happily ever after.

Take note that this is just an example of a skeletal outline. It may be shorter or even much longer than this. The important thing is to plot the story and the events properly. It is also worth noting that this kind of outline is not just applicable to fiction writing. You can also use it for non-fiction works. This will be discussed in more detail later in the book.

A good thing about this approach is that it allows you to see the structure of your book more clearly. Usually, a skeletal outline clearly divides the book into parts and is just composed of single lines. When taken together, they all compose a whole story.

Bullet outline

- A bullet outline is one of the most common types of outlining. In fact, this is one that is widely used by people even if they do not read about it. With a bullet outline, you simply have to make notes in bullet form as to what will happen in the story. For example:

- Lisa is an accountant.

- One day, she meets Mr. Gibson, a high-stakes gambler.

- They get to know each other better.

- They fall in love with each other.

- However, Mr. Gibson's gambling addiction starts to become a problem and begins to affect their relationship.

- Lisa tries to help Mr. Gibson and does her best to save their relationship.

- (and so on and so forth)

This is an example of a bullet outline. So, how do you use this outline? It is actually fairly simple. Using the example, at first you expound on the part of the outline that says, "Lisa is an accountant." A good way to do this when you actually write your novel is to describe the nature of Lisa's work. Make it as meaningful and interesting as possible.

If you look at the next part of the sample outline, the next part is "One day, she meets Mr. Gibson, a high-stakes gambler." Of course, you would not have to write this line as is. Rather, just like the first bullet, you make it more details. How did they meet? Perhaps Mr. Gibson starts to have money problems and needs an accountant to save his business. You can explore and expound on this once you actually start to write the book. Take note that this single bullet alone can take a whole chapter. This is just to give you an example of how to use a bullet outline more effectively.

A bullet outline is a very simple yet effective method. Another benefit of using this kind of outline is that it gives you a lot of room to exercise your imagination once you start to write the story. The outline focuses more on the flow of the story instead of what is actually happening in the story.

It is common to use a bullet outline on a per chapter basis. Many writers first prepare an outline in bullet form before they begin writing a chapter. This way, they can be sure that they know the direction of the story. Every bullet point is also usually short, so it would not be hard for you to follow it. Once you have a well-established outline in bullet form, then all you need to do is fill in the details of every bullet point and not worry about the direction that your story will take.

Chapter outline

A chapter outline divides a story into chapters. Every chapter will then have an outline of what is going to happen in that particular chapter. Here is an example:

Chapter 1: The Meeting

Noah calls for all the soldiers to attend the secret meeting.

Every soldier attends the meeting, except for Jason.

Jason, the number one soldier in the world, wakes up in a hospital with amnesia.

Even though Jason is not able to attend the meeting set by Noah, Noah is soon able to follow his tracks and visits him in the hospital.

Noah reminds Jason who he really is.

As you can see from the example, the book will be divided into chapters and every chapter will then be divided into sub-topics or events that take place in the story. A chapter outline is a good method, especially if you are particular with every chapter in your book.

As is usual, only the main points are included. This is to give room for you to exercise your creative imagination when you write the story. The outline is just enough to guide you as to what will happen next and avoid the situation where you get stuck up not knowing how to make the story to flow continuously. A chapter outline is also one that is commonly used by writers.

Sequence outline

A sequence outline puts more focus upon the sequencing of the events in the story. However, it still outlines the important points, so even this method alone would be enough to help you with writing your book. Here is an example of this kind of outline:

1 - Dianne, still a very young child, is baptized as a witch.

2 - Her parents were killed for practicing sorcery.

3 - She soon grows into one of the most powerful witches.

4 - Dianne meets King Gregory, the man who had ordered for her parents to be burned at the stake.

(and so on and so forth)

As you can see, there is a fine outline of the sequence of the events. If you are the type of writer who finds it hard to stick to the flow of your story, then a sequence outline may be the one for you.

Although you can add in as many details as you want, it is important to stick to the sequence; otherwise, a change may have major effects on the story as a whole. Take note that if you mess up with even just one part of the sequence, then you should check how it affects the other parts. Are they still logical enough when taken together? This method is also commonly used by writers. It is also like a bullet form outline but is more particular with the sequence of the events and the flow of the story.

Flowchart outline

This approach makes use of a flowchart. This is similar to a sequence outline but makes use of a chart that is also in proper sequence. Here is a simple example:

Adam works as a painter --> He attends an event for artists --> While at the event, he sees and meets Stella --> He falls in love with her at first sight --> and so on and so forth.

As you can see, the scenes or parts of the chapters are reflected through this flowchart. When you finally start working on the book, then you will add in the details to every point in the chart. A single part of the flowchart can cover a few pages up to a whole chapter, depending on what is happening in your story. So, for example, let us take the first part of the flowchart: Adam works as a painter. When you write this in your book, you can then expound on this topic. You describe the nature of his work and you can also write and show what happens in his life as a painter. As you can see, just these things alone can take many pages, even a whole chapter.

The thing with a flowchart method, just like any other outlining method, is for you to pinpoint the main parts of the story and ensure that you arrange things in the right order. Once everything is set, then you simply have to add the details when you write the book.

Visual outline

If you are fond of drawing, then this style of outlining may be the one for you. When you use a visual outline, all that you need to do is to draw the main events in a story, especially its plot. Take note that instead of writing in words, this approach lies in drawing and making figures. For this, you may want to use a notebook. You can fill each page with a drawing that would illustrate what the scene will be. You then follow it up with another scene on the next page, and so on and so forth.

Even if you cannot draw well, you can still use this approach. After all, just like any other outlines, this is something that you do not need to show to anyone else. An advantage of using drawings instead of words in making an outline is that you will have more room to play with the words, as well as for the exercise of your imagination. This is because every drawing can have diverse meanings and significance. If you want a style of outline that will give you maximum use of your imagination once you begin writing your book, then perhaps using a visual outline is a good idea. However, the drawback is that this kind of outlining may not always work for everyone. In fact, the very reason why you want to make an outline is to have a good sense of direction when you finally write your book. The risk is that you may not be so inspired when you finally write your book that the drawings may start to look boring or empty to you.

Chapter 3: Non-Fiction Outline

Pure summary

Just like for fiction writing, you can also use the pure summary approach for non-fiction book writing. When you use this approach, simply make a summary of the information. This means that you do not have to explain anything. Just make a summary of every chapter in the book. For sub-topics, you can simply write a one or two-sentence summary. Again, this is just a summary, so there is no need for you to expound or explain anything. Still, it is worth noting that when you read a summary, the stories must be coherent and logical enough. In other words, it must still be a complete story with proper flow and structure. However, of course, you do not want for it to too detailed. After all, it is just a summary, which can be a summary per chapter or even per sub-topic in every chapter. The important thing is for the summary to mention the main points of the book. This will also ensure that you will not forget about them.

When you use this method, then it is also important that you pay attention to the sequence of the information. A common rule in non-fiction writing is to start from the basics, and then gradually branch out to more complicated matters on the subject.

In non-fiction, you are not expected to make a well-detailed summary considering that there is a chance that you still need to learn more specific details about the topic in question. Of course, if you know exactly what you are writing about then you may only require a minimum level of research; however, if you are writing something about which you do not have enough knowledge, then there would be little that needs to be summarized. If you want, you can just research and study the subject first before you start to make a pure summary outline. However, do not let the lack of research prevent you from using this approach. After all, you have the convenience of having open books and information both when you make an outline and when you write the book.

Skeletal outline

A skeletal outline is common in non-fiction writing, especially when the book deals with a technical topic. This is because a skeletal outline offers exactly what you would need for non-fiction writing. When you use this approach, you begin with a subtitle, which may be the name of your chapter. You then identify and specify the skeletal outline of the book with the topics and sub-topics that you will discuss in the book. Needless to say, this follows the same format as the one for fiction. However, unlike a fiction book, this does not follow any plot. Rather, it has a more logical flow to it. For example, when you write a book about bitcoin, you should not talk about bitcoin mining right away. Instead, you should start with the basics, such as what bitcoin is, what a cryptocurrency is, and others, and then make your way up from there.

Bullet outline

A bullet outline is excellent when you deal with specifics. For example, when you make an outline of a chapter or sub-chapter in a book. Also, what you can do is to highlight the name of a chapter, and then simply outline in bullet form what you want to talk about for that part of the book. For example, let us say that you want to write a book about the cryptocurrency Bitcoin, here is a sample outline:

Chapter 1: The Basics of Bitcoin

- What is Bitcoin?

- What is cryptocurrency?

- What is a cryptocurrency wallet?

- Who uses bitcoin

- How does a bitcoin transaction work?

- (and others)

As you can see, every point is made clear. All that is left for you to do is add the details. Of course, you can further use the bullet outline like this:

Chapter 1: The Basics of Bitcoin

- What is Bitcoin?

    - a digital money

    - uses cryptography

- What is cryptocurrency?

    - cryptography for secure communication and transaction

- What is a cryptocurrency wallet?

    - a place to store cryptocurrency

    - kinds of cryptocurrency wallets (hot and cold wallets)

- Who uses bitcoin

- anyone with an Internet connection

- How does a bitcoin transaction work?

    - Input

    - Recipient's wallet address

    - Amount

As you can see, this makes it more detailed and it will be easier to fill in the information once you start writing the book. When you write non-fiction, outlining your work is more practical. After all, non-fiction works do not deal so much with one's creative imagination. The important thing is for you to be able to cover the technical details and be able to present them effectively.

Chapter outline

A chapter outline is one of the simplest ways to make an outline for a non-fiction book. Basically, you simply have to write the name of the chapter, and then add in the titles of the sub-topics within a chapter. This is also like a bullet form of outlining but is more general. Of course, you can also make it more specific by further outlining the sub-topics just like in a bullet outline. In fact, both kinds of outline are very similar to each other.

The first step in a chapter outline is to set the titles of the chapters. Again, as a rule in non-fiction, you should start with the basics. The reason is that you must first establish a foundation for your readers before you delve into more complicated matters. A common mistake committed by writers is to assume that the reader already knows and understands the topic. If you come to think of it, this understanding is highly flawed. After all, a reader would not have to waste time reading your book if he is already aware or if he already understands what is written in your book. So, never assume that the reader can easily understand what you write. Instead, have an open mind and consider the reader as someone who knows nothing about your subject. Of course, this is subject to some exceptions, for example, if you target readers are really those who already have an idea of your subject. A good example of this will be the advanced guides or manuals.

Once you have the titles of the different chapter ready, then it is time for you to add in the subtitles that will be placed under each corresponding chapter. You should be careful about the subtitles because they are the ones that will lead the development of the book. Hence, they are the ones that will form the structure of the book. Just stick to the basic rule of starting with the basics and then work your way up, and you will be fine. This is just a matter of presentation. Feel free to try different combinations until you find the one that feels most natural and convenient for a reader.

The number of chapters will depend on the kind of book that you write, as well as the number of words of the entire book. Normally, the longer the book is, the more chapters it will include. When you write your outline, be sure to pay attention to how many chapters your book will have, as well as the number of sub-topics that you will be using. It helps if you have more sub-topics so that you will not run out of things to write about. However, take note that book writing is not about the length but the quality if your book. Hence, it is important that you focus more on the quality of your writing that on the number of chapters or subtitles that your book has.

Research

Although not considered as a complete outlining method, when it comes to non-fiction writing, research is the main tool that you have in your arsenal. Although you are still free to use your imagination, non-fiction writing has certain restraints upon one's writing. The golden rule is that you cannot contradict a fact. Well, except, of course, if you have another set of facts to present that can support your view. Take note that when it comes to non-fiction writing, the facts are your friends. Needless to say, in a non-fiction book, almost everything that you write should be backed up by research or at least verifiable. This is to make your writing more believable and credible.

In non-fiction writing, it does not matter how good your outline is if you do not understand the subject. Hence, make sure that you have all the necessary materials to get to know your subject and do as much research as possible. The more that you know your subject, the easier it will be for you to come up with a good outline, and the easier it will be for you to complete the book.

Chapter 4: Best Practices

Know your characters

When you write a story, especially in fiction writing, it is important for you to know your characters. It is worth noting that an outline is not something that you use to get to know your characters. It is important for you to know the characters first before you make an outline.

Take note that the characters are important as they are the ones that tell and develop the story. If there are not enough characters or if you do not know your characters well enough, then the story will not grow properly. Therefore, is important for you to know and understand who your characters are. In fact, once you know your characters, then telling the story will come naturally as the characters themselves will play out the story. This is the part of writing a story where the writer becomes a mere observer of his characters. You can allow your characters to lead you. This will give you an idea of what the story will be and, so it will be easier for you to make an outline.

If you do not know your characters yet, especially your main characters in the story, then you should give yourself more time to get to know them. You do not necessarily have to know all your characters completely. You will know if you already have sufficient understanding of your characters when the characters themselves are able to lead and create the story for you. Needless to say, every character must have his or her own persona and should act according to that personality.

A suggested way to know your characters is to interview them one by one. This is a common practice used by novel writers. So, how does it work? Just imagine talking to your character. Ask them questions and see and feel how they respond. This may seem strange to some people, but many writers use this approach. They talk to their characters to the point like they feel that they are merely recording (writing) what the characters in the story are telling them. Once characters are given a persona and existence in the story, it will seem that they really have an identity and life of their own. Hence, talk with your characters and ask them questions. Learn from them. This way you will be more able to develop your story.

Know your story

Take note that your plot is like the skeleton of your story. Therefore, when you write a plot it is also important that you already have an idea of what your story is going to be. When you write an outline, it is not important for you to know the minor details and the dialogues of the characters. However, it is important for you to know the main points of your story or the main events that will shape your story. These are the things that will constitute your outline.

The more that you know your story, the easier it will be for you to make an outline of it. After all, making an outline is as simple as recording essential details and skipping dialogues and other things that are considered important to a novel. It is more focused on simply having a worthwhile story instead of discussing all the things that happen in a story.

Now, it is also worth noting that many writers write an outline even without knowing their story. How is this possible? Well, they allow the process of outlining to reveal the story to them. To do this, you just need a basic idea. You write it down as part of an outline, and then simply add more details to it to continue to grow your idea. Since you are just making an outline, it does not have to be too detailed, and you should just focus on the main points that will help develop the story.

Keep it simple

It is important to keep your outline simple. Remember that your outline should not be a cage that will limit your imagination. Rather, it should serve as a guide that will help you come up with a meaningful story. Therefore, keep your outline simple, including only the main and important points that should be in your story.

As a rule, small or minor details should not be placed in an outline, except if they are important to the story. The reason why you do not include everything in your outline is to prevent the outline from limiting you to exercise your imagination as you write your story. Again, an outline should only serve as a guide.

You also do not have to make your outline beautifully worded. Do not forget that the outline is only for your own eyes, so you do not have to spend so much effort in finding the right combination of words. You can save such effort for when you finally write the book. Instead of worrying about the words that you use, focus on the story that you want to tell, as well as the flow of the events and information.

Be flexible

It is worth remembering that an outline only functions as a guide. As such, it is not required for you to always stick to your outline. This is important for you to remember, especially if you suddenly come up with a better idea than the one in your outline while writing the story. This is another reason why you should keep your outline as simple as possible. By keeping it simple and just including the important parts of the story, then you will have more room to exercise your imagination.

It is considered very common for writers to suddenly stray away from their original outline. This is why you should not spend so much time worrying about how your outline is written. After all, it is still just a guide for you; and being the writer, you are free not to follow your outline.

Flexibility is important. Normally, the story only reveals itself fully even to the writer only when you actually pen down the story. This may sometimes come as a surprise, even to the author himself. As you write your book, the more you realize what the story is really all about. Simply put, as you follow your outline, you are also led to discover more about it. Now, from time to time, you may have to change course and take a completely different one than what you have originally outlined. This is normal, but just be sure to take a better path than the previous or current one. Also, if you ever change your course, you may want to stop for a while and reflect on the direction of your new outline.

A normal part of flexibility is to be flexible enough to update your outline. Yes, an outline can undergo so many changes and modifications as you write your book. Take note that you do not need to write new outlines, rather you can just edit your current outline little by little.

A common mistake committed by writers is to change a part in an outline and then allow the new storyline to lead the way without him knowing where it will actually go. Then this happens, then it is as good as writing without an outline. Now, I am not saying that this approach is wrong. Again, there are no hard and fast rules about how to write a book. However, if you are the type who cannot write properly and organize your thoughts without a guide, then what you should do in this case is to update your outline. Yes, updating an outline is something that you should do every time you make even minor changes to your outline. The outline must remain logical and coherent all throughout. This will ensure that your novel or the story itself will also be logical, coherent, and well structured. After all, your very story is just the outline itself, only that it now has more details. For example, if your outline says that Samantha is beautiful, then your story will make descriptions or show certain scenes to show just how beautiful she is. Still, the very essence of the writing can be traced back to your simple outline. Outlining and being flexible go hand in hand. Although there are writers who stick completely to their original outline and do not let anything divert their path (which is not wrong per se), sometimes it is good to be more open and allow changes to take place, especially positive changes.

Have a clear premise

Even before you work on an outline, you should first establish your premise. Ask yourself:

- Who is/are my main character/s in the story?

- Where does the story take place? In what year or time?

- What is the conflict in the story?

- What will be the turning point of my story?

- What message do I want the story to communicate to the readers?

- Who will be the enemies in the story, if any?

Once you have answered all these questions, then it means that you have a good idea of what your story will be. Take note that these are just basic questions. You are free to expound and ask more specific questions. But, these questions will reveal to you the premise of your story or what it is really about. Now, in case you find it hard to answer these simple questions, then it only means that you need to think about your story even more. Do not forget that an outline can only be made if you have a story to tell. Although an outline does not need a complete story, it requires that its essential elements should be present.

When you ask yourself these questions, it is important that you be completely honest with yourself. It is unfortunate that some writers delude themselves and hate saying" I don't know." Take note that this is a normal part of the writing process. The more that you admit to yourself the parts in your story that are still unclear to you, then the more you will understand what your story is really about. After all, the act of writing is still an act of self-discovery. You do not need to have the answers right away. It is normal to accept that you do not know the answers to some questions; the important thing is not to stop to seek for an answer. Of course, to do this, you need to reflect and delve more into your story.

Take a break

Just as you take some breaks to finish writing a book, you should also give yourself time to take a break when you are working on an outline. It is not uncommon for professional writers to spends days just to work on their outline. If you are just starting out to learn how to write and use an outline, then feel free to take as much time as you need. Just do not forget that an outline should make the writing of the book to easier in the long run. Unfortunately, some writers get too caught up writing their outlines that they fail to even start writing the actual book.

You will also be able to think much more clearly and be more creative if you allow your mind to relax. In fact, writers are strongly advised to give themselves a break from time to time even while working on the actual book. It is not uncommon to find writers who go to the beach and spend time on vacation while working on a book. This is because you will be a much more effective writer when you allow yourself to rest. With a fresh and rejuvenated mind, you will be able to use your creative talent more effectively.

Choose and organize your ideas

A book comes from an outline. But, where does an outline come from? Yes – an outline comes from ideas. However, it is worth noting that in the process of writing a book, it is very common to experience being bombarded with lots of ideas. For example, let us take a simple example where you present a protagonist in a story. Let us say that your hero is a man who happens to work in secret service for the government. There are tons of different ideas that you can use to show this. There are also many ways by which the story can go. Does he have super powers? Is he going to die and then resurrect? Or is he just an ordinary person who just happens to be good at what he does or maybe he is not even good at his job and merely relies on luck. The thing is that although outlining is a way to record and organize your ideas, you should also choose the ideas that you will be using in your story.

Now, once you have organized the ideas in your mind, it will then be easy for you to plot your story by making an outline. It is simply hard to make an outline when you know that you yourself do not know your story.

Observe proper sequence

When you write your way outline, it is important for you to pay attention to the proper sequence of the events or information. If it is a fiction book, I then the building and arrangement of the story should be in proper order. If you are writing a non-fiction book, then the information should be in an ordered sequence that will make the information more understandable to your audience. This is important especially if you are writing about a technical topic. For a fiction book, you should build up the story from beginning up to the end. In case of a non-fiction book, then you should share the information by starting from the basic details, and then continue building your way up to more complicated topics or sub-topics in the book.

Making an outline is the best way to set the proper sequencing of events of your story. Unfortunately, some writers still write the bulk of words only to end up with a confusing storyline. By making an outline, you can easily work on the sequence of the events of your story. In fact, you will be able to view and imagine your story completely, and all that will be left for you to do is to add in the details.

If you ever find yourself having a hard time putting things in the right sequence of ideas or events, then it is usually a sign that you should pause for a while and try to understand what is really going on in your story. Sometimes the logical sequence itself will be the one to guide you as to what to write next.

Focus on the main points

Making an outline is simply making a list of the important points of the book in proper order. You should focus on the main points. For a fiction book, the main points will be the beginning of the story, the rising action, climax, falling action, and the denouement. In the case of a non-fiction book, the main points, of course, would relate to the important details regarding your subject.

It is worth noting that some minor details may also be considered a necessary element in the development of a story. In this case, you can include the said minor details in your outline.

But, what are the main points? How do you know if a certain detail should be considered a main point and be included in your outline or not? Well, it depends. If the detail or information is something that is important in building up the story, then it is to be considered a main point and should be included in your outline. However, if it is something that your book or story can do without, then it is just a minor detail. The important thing about making an outline is to give you a good sense of direction. It has to function as a logical road map of your thoughts even if you forget about your story. After all, it is not uncommon for writers to think of an exciting plot only to have it slip away before they are able to get it written down completely. Whenever this happens, a possible wonderful story is lost to the world.

It does not have to be perfect

An outline does not need to be perfect. Keep in mind that it is just a guide. Hence, there is no need to follow it to the letter. Even if you come up with what you believe to be a perfect outline, know that it is still just an outline. As such, you should not allow yourself to be limited by it.

It is also worth noting that no matter how perfect you think your outline is, there is still a chance that it may be revised or modified. This is true, especially in the case of novels. It is not uncommon for writers to start at something specific only to be taken by the story somewhere more beautiful than they had imagined before writing the book. Does this mean that writing an outline is not important? Of course not. An outline assures that you maintain sense and direction in your story. However, it is worth noting that it considered common for writers to make changes to their outline several times as they write the book. Now, you should be careful when you do this. As a general rule, you should not change your original outline. You must stick to it. However, as an exception, you may change your outline if you are able to come up with a better version of the story. It has to make the story more exciting or meaningful for the readers. If not, then you need to stick to your outline. This is the reason why you should not aim to have a perfect outline because such a thing simply does not exist.

Although you do not expect an outline to be perfect, it does not mean that the outline can just contain every thought that you think would be good for your story. An outline must still be carefully written. How can you expect for your outline to guide you if the ideas do not match up well with one another or if the outline itself fails to follow a logical sequence? Hence, it is important that you work on your outline, but do not aim for perfection. Having the right ideas and correct flow would be enough.

Now, just because an outline does not have to be perfect does not mean that you should not give it as much time as it deserves. The outline, after all, serves as the foundation of your book. Therefore, take as much time as you need when making your outline, which leads us to the next topic: time.

Remember that an outline is just a guide

Although an outline can be regarded as important, do not forget the fact that an outline is still just your guide. Therefore, you are free to stick to it while you write the book or totally abandon it halfway. However, this does not mean that an outline is no longer important. But, you need to understand this so that you will not end up like other writers who get too obsessed with their outline.

Remember to see and use your outline as a guide in writing the book. You are always free to change or revise your outline as many times as you want and in any way that you deem best.

Take your time

When making an outline, you should take as much time as you need. Although your outline will not be a part of your book, it is still the foundation of your book. Consider it like a business plan or blueprint of your masterpiece.

Although you can make an outline in as fast as a few minutes, it is not uncommon for professional writers to spend even a week to work on an outline. This is true, especially if you want to create a high-quality book.

You should also learn to organize and manage your time. Unfortunately, there are many writers who commit the mistake of procrastinating. The temptation to procrastinate is something that you should watch out for when you write a book. A good way to avoid procrastination is to set daily objectives. For example, aim to be able to finish 15% of your outline every day. Also, take note that writing an outline is just part of the process. The more important part is for you to write your book, which will take more time and effort than writing an outline.

Have your sources ready

This is true, especially if you work on a non-fiction book. You should have your sources ready. This is because sometimes it is hard to look for your sources during the time of actual writing. A good way to keep your outline more organized is to cite your sources in the outline. One of the main reasons for using an outline is to make the work of writing the book easier for you.

You do not have to cite your sources formally. After all, the outline is your own private document. You do not need to show it to your readers or anyone else. The purpose of having your sources ready and to cite your sources is for you to be ready when you write your book. So that when you write the book, you will know exactly where to look for information as you fill in every major and minor topic in your outline. Even fiction writers can use the same approach. After all, many fiction stories also incorporate real-life events. Take, for example, *Da Vinci Code*, which combines fiction with non-fiction information.

When it comes to writing non-fiction, it is important to take note that you should stick to the facts. If you want to force your creative thought and ideas into the page, then you might want to consider shifting to fiction writing. It is worth noting that readers of non-fiction books read not mainly for entertainment or pleasure, but to get as much as useful information as possible. They do not care about your opinions unless your views have a good basis and foundation. Hence, it is important to identify the kind of genre that you want to write in even before you make an outline. This is because the style of writing and even the expectation of the readers have certain distinctions between fiction and non-fiction writing. As for the sources, be sure to quote from credible sources. If possible, use internationally known and accepted formats like APA or Chicago when citing your sources.

Ask yourself questions

Okay, so now you have a clear idea of how to make an outline. But, how do you know which types to include in your outline? The key is to ask yourself questions, the right questions. For example, when writing fiction, let us say that you have a character named Max. Now, ask yourself, who is Max? Let us say that Max is a poet.

Ask yourself who is Max as a poet? What is he like? Once you are able to answer this then you can have something to place in your outline: Max is a poet who writes for a princess who does not even know that he loves her. Next, ask yourself what happens next. You may come up with the next part of the outline, like: A big event is about to take place and Max and the princess are going to attend the said event. The next step is for you to imagine the event and ask yourself what happens to Max at the event, and so on and so forth. As you can see, by simply asking yourself the right questions, you can develop a story.

How about for non-fiction writing? Well, a similar technique can be used. However, if you are dealing with a technical topic, let us say a book about Blockchain technology, then you should ask a different kind of questions. For example: What is blockchain? What are the types of blockchain? What is the history of blockchain? This continues until you come up with a highly informative book.

It is important to ensure that every part of your outline should help develop or enhance the book. This way you can be sure that your book will be interesting and informative.

Okay, so how do you know the right questions to ask? It is simple. You just have to take the perspective of a reader who does not know your book or subject. Therefore, if it is fiction writing or when you write a novel, if you have a character in mind named Gabriel, then ask: Who is Gabriel? What does he do? Where does he live? All these questions will soon open up a whole new story that is full of meaning and value. Now, in the case of non-fiction writing, again just consider that a reader is a beginner in the subject that you are discussing. Therefore, you should start with the basic details and lay down a good foundation. After which, you can then talk about more complicated topics within your subject matter.

Practice

When it comes to learning how to outline properly and more effectively, nothing beats practice. So, if you want to learn how to make an outline, then just start practicing it. Make an outline for the next books that you write. No matter how much you read about it, it remains true that the only way for you to appreciate and realize just how beneficial making an outline can be.

Learning how to write a good outline is just like learning to write good books. This means that you simply have to practice it by applying it regularly. If you get good at writing outlines, then the task of writing a book becomes simpler and more manageable.

You do not have to learn the different ways to outline a book. After all, when you make an outline, you only need to use one method. If you want, you can combine two methods at once. There is no strict rule as to when a particular method should be used over another. Therefore, feel free to use the one that you are most comfortable with.

Indeed, there are some writers who do not like the idea of using an outline. It is worth noting that this book does not make it a requirement or an obligation of a writer to use an outline, but merely shares how helpful an outline can be in the process of writing a book. Therefore, if you strongly prefer not to use an outline, then you are free to do so. In the world of book writing, whether or not you use an outline does not matter in the end. What matters is the final product, which is the book itself. There are writers who use an outline and know for sure how useful it is, while there are those who simply allow the story to unfold like a surprise. The only disadvantage of not having an outline is that it is common to follow a story only to meet a dead end or you just realize that the story has become dull and boring.

An outline assures that before you even start working and writing your boo, you are assured of a good sense of direction. All you need to do is write, and even if all that you do is to stick to your outline and not change any parts of the story but merely add in the details pursuant to your outline, then you can be sure that you will end up with a good book, provided that you have prepared a good outline.

Once again, it is up to you as a writer whether or not to use an outline. The best way to find out what works for you would be to give it a try. Write a book without an outline and then write one that has a proper outline, and see which writing experience is better for you. In the end, it is not about whether or not you have used an outline, but how much the book has made your soul grow in the process.

Conclusion

Thanks for making it through to the end of this book. We hope it was informative and able to provide you with all of the tools you need to achieve your goals whatever they may be.

The next step is to apply everything that you have learned and start making an outline of your book. Learning how to make an outline is one of the best things that should be in the arsenal of every writer. It is useful and makes the book writing process easy and manageable.

If you are a beginner, you might encounter some difficulties writing an outline for the first time. The key is to not be too strict about it. It is worth noting that the methods revealed in this book are also just guides. You, as the writer, has all the right to make your own modifications. In fact, you may want to develop your own way of making an outline. The important thing is for you to know and understand how to use it to help you in writing a book. Keep in mind that there is really no right and wrong way of making an outline as long as it is able to help you write your book. After all, the very purpose of an outline is to help a writer and make the process of writing a book simpler, easier, and more organized.

When you write a book, it is not uncommon to suddenly feel so lost. Some writers have a story to tell but do not know how to start or how to maintain a smooth flow of the pages. This is why making an outline is important. There is a big universe out there, and you need to place only the right stuff into your book in proper order. Indeed, the task of a writer is not an easy thing. But, if you learn how to use an outline, then you have an invaluable weapon that you can use to make the writing process so much easier.

Good luck!